EFFECTIVE
STEWARDSHIP

Participant's Guide

DOING WHAT MATTERS MOST

EFFECTIVE
STEWARDSHIP

Participant's Guide

Jonathan and Amanda Witt

ZONDERVAN.com/
AUTHORTRACKER
follow your favorite authors

ZONDERVAN

Effective Stewardship Participant's Guide
Copyright © 2009 by Acton Institute

Requests for information should be addressed to:

Zondervan, *Grand Rapids, Michigan 49530*

ISBN 978-0-310-32229-0

Interior design by Matthew Van Zomeren

Printed in the United States of America

09 10 11 12 13 14 15 16 17 • 24 23 22 21 20 19 18 17 16 15 14 13 12 11 10 9 8 7 6 5 4 3 2 1

God has entrusted us with aptitudes and abilities, and as good stewards, we must use them for his glory and not our own. This is true not only of musical, artistic, athletic, academic, business, and persuasive talents, but also of the spiritual gifts we have received.

—Kenneth Boa, *Conformed to His Image*

CONTENTS

How to Use This Participant's Guide

We're glad you've chosen to study the *Effective Stewardship* DVD curriculum. Ideally, anyone leading a group through this curriculum will both watch the video clip and read the corresponding content in the participant's guide prior to the group session. The curriculum is easy to follow, so this preparatory work isn't essential. However, the extra time of reflection and preparation on the group leader's part could make for a more searching and fruitful group study.

Participant's Guide Contents

This participant's guide contains five sessions corresponding to the five video lessons on the DVD:

.   1. Our Talents and Skills
    2. The Environment
    3. Loving Our Neighbor
    4. Church and Family
    5. Finances and Giving

Each session contains several parts:

Key Issue

This section briefly discusses the key scriptural insights related to the session topic.

DVD Teaching Notes

This short section lists some of the key themes from the DVD lesson and provides some space for taking notes.

Group Discussion Questions

This section is divided into three focus areas: DVD Discussion, Bible Exploration, and Living the Truth. The questions begin by focusing on the video clip, move to Scripture, and end with personal application and action. Interspersed throughout the discussion questions are quotes on the session topic by influential individuals both contemporary and historical.

Digging Deeper

For those who would like to further investigate this topic on their own, this section contains material adapted from the *NIV Stewardship Study Bible*, provided by the study Bible's general editor, Stephen Grabill. Much of the material from the study Bible was excerpted from other books on biblical stewardship.

Reading Resources

Each session closes with a list of recommended books and other resources for exploring the issue of biblical stewardship in greater depth.

Session One

OUR TALENTS AND SKILLS

Genesis 1:27; Matthew 25:14–30

> Again, it will be like a man going on a journey, who called his servants and entrusted his property to them. To one he gave five talents of money, to another two talents, and to another one talent, each according to his ability. Then he went on his journey.
>
> —*Matthew 25:14–15*

KEY ISSUE

Effective stewardship extends to our daily vocation, using our God-given talents to serve God in the work we have been given.

We're accustomed to thinking that some people are creative, and some are not. But in Genesis, when we're told that God made us in his image, what do we know about God? Up to that point in the Bible, all we know about God is that he creates good things. The implication is profound: Being made in God's image means we have been made to be creative—not to create out of nothing as God can, but to create by transforming the world in good ways.

If your sphere of influence is the home, you're called to creatively transform that space into a better place. Whether your sphere is business, industry, the service sector, education, or some other profession, you're called to use your creativity to make that world a better place.

Wherever you are, however large or small your sphere of influence, you are responsible for actively and creatively using your talents and resources. Our Master has entrusted each of us with talents and resources, and he expects us to use them to good effect. We are warned against being merely passive onlookers in life (Matt. 25:14–30; Mark 13:32–37). And Jesus reminds us: "From everyone who has been given much, much will be demanded; and from the one who has been entrusted with much, much more will be asked" (Luke 12:48). As Rev. Robert Sirico says, "We owe something to someone outside of ourselves with regard to how creative we are."

DVD TEACHING NOTES

We are all stewards

Made in the image of a creative God

Gnosticism and the incarnation

Christianity helped the West leap forward

Good works by the grace of God

GROUP DISCUSSION QUESTIONS

DVD Discussion

1. What images or thoughts come to mind when you hear the word *stewardship*? In your own words, what does it mean to be a "steward"?

> When the Possessor of heaven and earth brought you into being, and placed you in this world, he placed you here, not as a proprietor, but as a steward. As such he entrusted you, for a season, with goods of various kinds; but the sole property of these still rests in him, nor can ever be alienated from him.
> —*John Wesley*

2. Rev. Robert Sirico says, "We are all called to God ... each person has a unique work that only he or she can do." The word *vocation* comes from the Latin word, *vocare*, meaning "called." How would you describe your vocation or calling? List some of the different roles where you are called to be a steward of God's gifts and resources.

3. We often tend to divide our life into the spiritual and the secular. Dave Stotts reminds us: "There isn't just a God part of life and all the rest—it's all God's." Consider this quote from the theologian Abraham Kuyper: "There is not one square inch in all of creation about which Jesus Christ does not cry out: 'This is mine! This belongs to me.'" What do you think this quote suggests? Why is this important when we look at our roles and callings in life?

> Whether taking care of our toys at the age of four or managing the entire factory at the age of forty, if we do this work "as unto the Lord," God looks at our imitation of his sovereignty and his other attributes, and he is pleased. In this way we are his image-bearers, people who are like God and who represent God on the earth.
>
> —*Wayne Grudem*

4. Gnosticism separated the physical world from the spiritual world and taught that our spirituality has nothing to do with our day-to-day, physical existence. Where do you see examples of this way of thinking today?

How might this Gnostic influence lead us to downplay our responsibility to steward God's resources?

5. In the video clip, Rudy Carrasco reminds us that we will be called to give an account on the day of judgment for what we have done with the resources God has given us. Does this truth motivate you to be an effective steward? Why or why not?

Bible Exploration

Read together the parable of the talents in Matthew 25:14–30.

6. How did the owner distribute his wealth among the servants? Why were some given more than others?

7. How did each of the servants respond to the wealth he was given? What is the difference between the first two servants and the last servant?

8. The term *risk-taking* usually has negative connotations. Nobody wants his or her child to engage in "risky" behavior. Yet this parable condemns playing it safe with our God-given assets and celebrates certain types of risk-taking. God expects us to take prudent risks with the things he has lent us. What are some ways that we can take "risks" that honor God? What is the difference between a foolish risk and a responsible risk?

9. Why does the third servant bury the money he was given? How is his response shaped by his fear and lack of faith? In what way does fear keep us from being effective stewards of God's gifts to us?

10. What is the reward for faithful stewardship in this parable? What are the consequences of fearful stewardship?

11. Why do you think Jesus tells this parable? How would you apply its lesson to your own life?

Living the Truth

12. There may be times in your life when you don't feel you're using your talents much. Perhaps you're an artist or musician, but you've taken a salaried job to provide stability for your family. Perhaps you're a mother who has given up or limited your career in order to stay home with your children. Perhaps you've been laid off or forced to retire early from a job you loved, and now you're working odd jobs to fill your time or to make ends meet. Perhaps you've always found yourself in uninspiring jobs and see no prospect of more inspiring work on the horizon.

Do you believe it is possible to serve God through such work? If so, how?

> Work is the way we meet our basic needs. Work is also the way we express our basic nature as persons made in the image of God who is Creator. We cannot create out of nothing as God does, but we are made to trace the finger of God's intricate design in the material world and then use our creative abilities to reshape what the Creator has given us in order to produce cultures of glorious beauty and complexity.
>
> —*Ronald J. Sider*

13. In his book *Hearing God*, Dallas Willard emphasizes that this is our Father's world; we are safe here. "The promise," he says, "is not that God will never allow any evil to come to us but that no matter what befalls us, we are still beyond genuine harm due to the fact that he remains with us." Jesus himself describes many griefs that will come to Christians, and then says, "I have told you these things, so that in me you may have peace. In this world you will have trouble. But take heart! I have overcome the world" (John 16:33).

How might you make better use of your talents and other resources if you deeply believed that no real, lasting harm could ever come to you?

DIGGING DEEPER

> You may say to yourself, "My power and the strength of my hands have produced this wealth for me." But remember the LORD your God, for it is he who gives you the ability to produce wealth, and so confirms his covenant, which he swore to your forefathers, as it is today.
>
> —*Deuteronomy 8:17–18*

The message of Deuteronomy 8:10–18 couldn't be clearer—or more needed: God and God alone gives us the power to produce wealth. Even when our finances fluctuate between the extremes of affluence and poverty, we are called to unwavering trust and humility.

It should come as no surprise that God values industry and wealth creation, for God is the source and standard of both. Problems with wealth come when we allow ourselves to forget its source, driving us to look to false wellsprings of provision and security—the foundations of idolatry.

> Money provides many opportunities to glorify God: through investing and expanding our stewardship and thus imitating God's sovereignty and wisdom; through meeting our own needs and thus imitating God's independence; through giving to others and thus imitating God's mercy and love; or through giving to the church and to evangelism and thus bringing others into the kingdom.
>
> —*Wayne Grudem*

Take a moment to reflect on how exercising a God-given talent for business and entrepreneurship could lead to opportunities for evangelism (see Dan. 6:1–5).

Daniel, like Joseph before him, was entrusted with a distinguished position in a foreign kingdom. He executed well his duties as a leader, all the while showcasing the greatness of his God through his unflinching integrity and devotion.

Work is not a curse. There was work in the garden before Adam and Eve sinned. Human work and creativity are gifts from God. We are called to work creatively as we cultivate creation's potential (see Col. 1:15–20).

Jesus, the creator of all things, has "reconciled to himself all things" and is restoring and re-creating creation. He continues his creative work. Biblical stewards participate in that re-creation and restoration through our work on this earth, including our daily labor.

We not only share in God's creativity through our work, we also share God's sovereignty. Author Eugene H. Peterson calls all true work *king-work* to explain how our work is an extension of God's sovereign work:

> Work derives from and represents the sovereign God, who expresses his sovereignty as a worker: kingwork. Sovereigns work to bring order out of chaos; guard and fight for the sanctity of things and people; deliver victims from injustice and misfortune and wretchedness; grant pardon to the condemned and the damned; heal sickness; by their very presence bring dignity and honor to people and land. God's sovereignty isn't abstract—it's a working sovereignty and is expressed in work. All of our work is intended as an extension of and participation in that sovereignty.

Work is an honor and a privilege, a gift given to us by God. Everything we do, when guided by, and done for, the Lord, has meaning and value. As you use your gifts, talents, and resources this week, remember to thank the God who has blessed you with the skill and opportunity to serve him in your work.

READING RESOURCES

The Call of the Entrepreneur DVD (Grand Rapids: Acton Media, 2007).

The Entrepreneurial Vocation, by Robert A. Sirico (Grand Rapids: Acton Institute, 2002).

Leap Over a Wall: Earthy Spirituality for Everyday Christians, by Eugene H. Peterson (San Francisco: HarperOne, 1998).

The Mind of the Maker, by Dorothy L. Sayers (San Francisco: Harper One, 1987).

THE ENVIRONMENT

Genesis 1:26–28; Genesis 2:15–20; Psalm 8

> God blessed them and said to them, "Be fruitful and increase in number; fill the earth and subdue it. Rule over the fish of the sea and the birds of the air and over every living creature that moves on the ground."
>
> — *Genesis 1:28*

KEY ISSUE

Creation is not ours to use and abuse as we wish. Rather, we are stewards of God's creation.

A generation ago, the environmental movement was mainly about putting litter in its place and cleaning up the air and water. Today, however, many leading environmentalists treat nature as practically divine, and they see humans as parasites rather than as stewards of God's creation. Environmental scientist Eric Pianka, for instance, has spoken in positive terms about a killer disease wiping out "the scourge of humanity."

Former US Secretary of the Interior Don Hodel reminds us that responsible care for the environment will include placing a high priority on the most vulnerable humans on our planet. "If we do anything drastic," he says, "we will be affecting and killing people, starving people to death or causing disease in this next year or the year after that because … it's the people at the bottom of the economic pyramid who have no flexibility. They have no margin."

As Christians, we are called to care for God's creation, and that includes the crown of his creation: humanity. Care for the environment must be holistic, addressing both the long-term effects on our natural resources *and* the needs of people. Sacrificing the poor may seem like the easiest way to solve an environmental threat, but it's not good stewardship. Instead, we must use our God-given intellect and creativity to protect both the environment and other human beings.

DVD TEACHING NOTES

"The earth is the Lord's," not "the earth is the Lord"

Good intentions do not guarantee good results

Four questions about global warming

CO_2 caps and the poor

Humans are more than mouths

GROUP DISCUSSION QUESTIONS

DVD Discussion

1. Host Dave Stotts notes that some people see our earth as divine. How does this differ from the view of the Bible? What problems could such a view lead to, both in the way we treat the earth and in the way we treat our fellow humans?

> God designed this planet's environment just so we could live in it. We are the focus of his love and the most valuable of his creation.... God is not haphazard; he planned it all with great precision. The more physicists, biologists, and other scientists learn about the universe, the better we understand how it is uniquely suited for our human existence, custom-made with the exact specifications that make human life possible.
>
> *—Rick Warren*

2. Sometimes Christians are accused of not caring about the environment because they believe this world will one day be judged and destroyed, when Jesus returns. Former Secretary of the Interior Don Hodel mentioned a time when an earlier Secretary of the Interior was asked a loaded question: "Is the reason you don't care about conserving the environment because you believe in the second coming of the Lord?" If you had been asked this question, how would you have tried to answer it?

3. This session talks about the intense controversy surrounding global warming policies. Thoughtful consideration of this issue involves asking several questions.

- *Are human beings causing it?* Some scientists say global warming is caused by human being; others suggest it is due to natural causes related to solar radiation and changes in wind patterns.

- *Is the warming bad?* We need to ask: "What is the optimal temperature for the planet?" While warming may have some serious consequences, a warmer world may also have some benefits (longer growing seasons, increased food production).

- *Would any of the policies advocated make a difference?* Supporters of the Kyoto Protocol concede that even if every nation complied, the treaty would affect the global temperature by only about two tenths of a degree Fahrenheit by 2050. At the same time, full compliance would drive up the cost of energy, further impoverishing poor countries.

As a group, discuss your own views on this issue. How can we engage in a healthy, productive dialogue on this matter when disagreements arise among fellow Christians?

4. Fred Smith and Steven Hayward discuss how the well-intentioned Endangered Species Act unintentionally led to a phenomenon known as "shoot, shovel, and shut up." Instead of providing incentives to farmers who found an endangered species on their land, and rewarding them for responsible care of these creatures, the regulation inadvertently penalized farmers and tempted the landowners to cover up the evidence.

What are some examples of ways the government could reward a farmer in this situation?

Bible Exploration

Read together Genesis 1:26–28; 2:15–20; 3:17–19; and Psalm 8.

5. Some critics of Christianity have pointed to Genesis 1:28, where God gives human beings "dominion" over his creation, as evidence that the Bible is the cause of environmental problems. As we have learned, our "rule" of God's creation should be guided by the principle of responsible stewardship. Given this understanding, what does Genesis 1:26–28 actually teach about human beings and their responsibility toward the creation? What might this look like, practically?

6. According to Psalm 8, what is David's response as he considers our stewardship of God's creation? How should this inform our own response?

7. Genesis 2:15–20 suggests that God has also placed animals under our stewardship. Yet many people today believe that human beings are just another animal, and that other animals have the same innate rights as we have. What problems might arise if we view humans and animals as possessing equal rights and value?

What problems arise if we neglect our stewardship responsibility and use animals and their habitats however we please?

8. In Genesis 3:17–19, the ground is cursed because of man's sin, suggesting that our sin has a direct impact on the earth. We see that the land can suffer when man sins. Farmers who through impatience or greed fail to rotate their crops will eventually have barren fields. The factory owner who saves a buck by dumping waste into the river will eventually destroy the life in the river. Good environmental solutions will address the root problem—human sin. How does this understanding of the source of environmental problems help us in developing solutions? What factors need to be considered?

What is good health? God's Word uses the word *shalom* to mean peace, wholeness, soundness, well-being and good health. In the Old Testament, *shalom* is used when there is harmony between people and between people and things. To be in harmony means to live in peace with someone or something. To be in good health, a person must live in harmony. But with whom must we live in harmony? First God, then oneself, then others, then nature.

—*Stan Rowland*

9. Some in the environmental movement discourage having children because it just means more mouths consuming our planet's resources. They believe population control is a good environmental policy. Others argue that humans are creators, not just consumers, and that the world could use more good biblical stewards.

Psalm 127:3–5 says that children are a blessing from the Lord, and Genesis 1:28 tells us that we are to be "fruitful and multiply, and fill the earth" (NRSV). How does the Bible inform our perspective on this issue? As Christians, how should we respond?

Living the Truth

10. Effective stewardship of the environment begins in our homes and neighborhoods. What are you doing to personally exercise good stewardship over God's creation? Discuss ways that Christians can model thoughtful and responsible action in this area.

The ground that feeds us lies quiet. As we walk on the grass, the earth feels like a sleeping giant, a friendly giant. The most frequent sounds from the inanimate world include the sounds of running water and the sound of the wind as it swishes through the trees. The air, soil, and water cannot protest when we dump chemicals into streams and rivers, when we bury harmful wastes, when we fill the air with toxic fumes. We exploit nature's silent vulnerability.

—*Eugene F. Roop*

11. As noted in this session, stewardship of the environment has implications for various public policy issues related to population and poverty, food, energy, water, and care for animals, including endangered species. Are there any environmental issues that are of particular interest or concern to you? If so, what have you done to get involved?

DIGGING DEEPER

> Behold, I will create new heavens and a new earth.
> —*Isaiah 65:17*

Isaiah 65 describes things after the return of Christ as a time and place of perfect stewardship. Things will no longer fall apart; creation, our families, human institutions, distribution of commodities, and so forth, will be in perfect balance. Our stewardship now should approximate the way stewardship will be performed at the end of days. A crucial point to remember is that even in the next life, we will be about the work of cultivating God's good earth.

God has entrusted us with the role of cultivating the earth to its fullest potential. This means exercising responsible, limited dominion over the vast resources he has put into our trust.

Effective stewardship of creation requires teaching; it is not automatic. Children, especially, must be taught that a fallen creation doesn't mean the world is ruined or somehow unimportant.

The day of the Lord's return is still in the future, but we are called right now to appreciate, enjoy, and care for the natural world. Yes, the physical environment has been marred and scarred by sin, but it has by no means been ruined. Creation is still good. Christian environmental educators Loren and Mary Ruth Wilkinson offer some advice to parents seeking to raise good environmental stewards. "It is important to be continually open to the wonder and beauty (as well as the complexity and the bewildering pain) of nonhuman creation," they write. They offer several suggestions for accomplishing this:

1. *Observe the world around you with new eyes.* See and begin to understand the seasonal growth of plants, the passing through of migratory birds, the kinds of insects on the screen at night, the changes in the weather, the planets and the phases of the moon; recognize in the hills, valleys, and plains of today the moraines, uplifts, and lava flows of the past. All these are ways of learning to live in wonder and curiosity at the marvel and diversity of creation.

2. *Plant a garden.* Gardens are—in addition to being an important supplement to diet and budget—an excellent way of learning (and teaching) lessons about the basic processes of life. Particularly if the garden is nourished by the composting of vegetable

wastes, a family has the opportunity to observe and nurture photosynthesis, growth, and decay.

3. *Care for a dog, a cat, or a goldfish.* This is a good way of learning how to care for living things generally.

4. *Range more widely into places where the processes of life have proceeded with little human interference.* Such contact with relatively wild areas serves as a reminder that creation proceeds with great vitality quite apart from our involvement in it.

This week, take some time to stop and appreciate the natural world that God has created. Wonder at the beauty and diversity of God's creation, and consider how you can exercise effective stewardship over the environment.

READING RESOURCES

Cornwall Alliance for the Stewardship of Creation, *www.cornwall alliance.org.*

Environmental Stewardship in the Judeo-Christian Tradition: Jewish, Catholic, and Protestant Wisdom on the Environment, edited by Jay W. Richards (Grand Rapids: Acton Institute, 2007).

Where Garden Meets Wilderness: Evangelical Entry into the Environmental Debate, by E. Calvin Beisner (Grand Rapids: Eerdmans, 1997).

Session Three

LOVING OUR NEIGHBOR

Matthew 7:12; Luke 10:25 – 37; 2 Thessalonians 3:6 – 13

> But a Samaritan, as he traveled, came where the man was; and when he saw him, he took pity on him. He went to him and bandaged his wounds, pouring on oil and wine. Then he put the man on his own donkey, took him to an inn and took care of him.
>
> —*Luke 10:33 – 34*

KEY ISSUE

We cannot ignore the reality of human suffering. We must respond with discernment and compassion, looking for effective ways to help those in need. We are called to responsibly care for our neighbors, loving them as we love ourselves.

In the parable of the prodigal son (Luke 15:11 – 32), we see how God is merciful to spiritual losers. In the parable of the lost sheep (Luke 15:1 – 7), we see how God actively seeks out the wayward. One lesson is hard to miss: charity isn't just for "decent folks."

At the same time, we need to be careful that our well-intentioned efforts don't do more harm than good. Giving a man a fish is easier than teaching him to fish. Encouraging dependency is easier than training up a dependable provider. While there are special situations that call for simple handouts, we must never forget that human beings are created in the image of God to be *creative*. Sometimes the best way to love someone is by holding them accountable and teaching them to embrace their God-given responsibilities. This is why Paul is being loving, not mean, when he says, "If a man will not work, he shall not eat" (2 Thess. 3:10b).

We also need to apply biblical principles to real-life problems in ways that can help those in developing countries. The spread of Christianity has done more to lift up the poor than any other force in history. History teaches us that centralized, state-run schemes to eliminate human misery usually end up creating even more misery. Benevolent aid to developing countries, though well-intentioned, rarely accomplishes what it is intended to do. As Christians, we need to promote solutions to global poverty that actually help poor countries move from poverty to prosperity.

DVD TEACHING NOTES
The Good Samaritan

A heart and mind for the poor

Always do that which ennobles people

Subsidiarity

What causes wealth?

GROUP DISCUSSION QUESTIONS

DVD Discussion

1. This video clip opened with a discussion of the parable of the Good Samaritan. With which of the characters in the story do you most identify? Who has been a "Good Samaritan" to you, caring for you in an unexpected way when you needed help?

2. Host Dave Stotts says, "Christians aren't called to random acts of kindness; we're called to truly help." What do you think he means by this statement?

Can you think of a situation where a person's random, charitable action might actually end up hurting a person, rather than helping them?

3. "Sometimes you injure with a helping hand." Consider the two examples mentioned in the video:

- Rudy Carrasco shared a story about a jobs training program where the standards of work were set very low, and kids were never fired from the program out of fear that they would end up back on the street. Years later, these same kids could not hold a job. They had never learned that breaking rules has consequences.

- Robert Woodson, president of the National Center for Neighborhood Enterprise, told how every year well-meaning people would donate toys for a Christmas program at a local women's shelter. But because volunteers handed out the toys to the children, it had the unintended effect of bypassing the parents, who were left out of the blessing of gift-giving.

What was the charitable goal in each situation? What was the unintended consequence that resulted from "good intentioned" help?

How could the program be changed to achieve the goal, without the unintended consequence?

4. Carrasco says, "In order to be effective [in helping the poor], it means that we're going to have to get very personally involved." To address a problem effectively, we need to be close to it, a concept known as *subsidiarity*. Subsidiarity suggests that the best solutions are developed by those most familiar with the problem. How have you seen this principle at work in your own life? What does it mean for us as we consider God's call to love those in need?

5. In the video, Robert Woodson argues that government-initiated welfare programs decimated families in African-American communities and created dependence on the state. Do you agree or disagree with his assessment of government welfare programs? Explain.

What problems are frequently created by government solutions to poverty? What role can the church have in addressing these problems and providing solutions?

6. Michael Miller of the Acton Institute says, "Many people ask what causes poverty, but I think the real question should be, what causes wealth?" What is the difference between these two perspectives and how might they lead to different solutions to the problem of poverty?

> Some Christians seem to wish to assume away certain economic laws when developing policies in areas such as the minimum wage or the provision of foreign aid. This is as sensible as assuming away the laws of gravity when considering the moral case for punishment by hanging.
>
> —*Phillip Booth*

Bible Exploration

7. Look up the following passages and summarize what each teaches about the poor:

• Psalm 140:12

• Proverbs 14:31

• Proverbs 19:17

• Galatians 6:9–10

8. Read Galatians 6:10 and Romans 12:13. These passages remind us of the priority of caring for the needs of those in our church family. What are some ways that churches can practice care for their own members?

How have you seen this practiced in your church?

9. In 2 Thessalonians 3:6–13, the apostle Paul writes about how we should treat those who are unwilling to accept responsibility for their own situation. How can this biblical principle inform our approach to caring for the poor, even as we seek to minister with love and compassion?

10. Read Matthew 25:31–46 and James 2:14–17. What do our efforts on behalf of those in need say about our faith, according to these passages?

If someone were to judge the vitality of your faith by this standard right now, how would you rate yourself on a scale of 1–5 (5 = very vital, 1 = anemic)?

11. How does the message of 2 Corinthians 8:9 and the example of Jesus inspire you to serve the poor?

The gospel speaks to you of a Redeemer who, although he was rich, became poor for your sake so he might make you rich. The gospel leads you to kneel down in worship before a child born to us, but born in a stable, laid down in a manger, and wrapped in swaddling clothes. It points you to God's Son, but one who became the *Son of Man* and went through the country, from wealthy Judea to the poorer, despised Galilee, addressing himself to those who were in need or oppressed by sorrow. Yes, it tells you that this singular Savior, before he left this earth, stooped before his disciples in the clothes of a slave, washed their feet one by one, and then stood and said, "For I have given you an example, that ye should do as I have done to you" (John 13:15).

—*Abraham Kuyper*

Living the Truth

12. Some Christians think their church should focus more on addressing the physical needs of the sick and poor. Others worry that undue stress on the "social gospel" may crowd out the gospel message.

    For the church, where is the biblical balance between addressing people's physical needs on the one hand and on the other, making disciples of all nations?

13. Not everyone who is in need is poor financially. Some are in need emotionally or socially, as is often the case with families broken by death or divorce. When James encouraged Christians to look after the orphans and widows (see James 1:27), he was calling attention to two groups who faced not only financial hardships but also the hardship of loneliness.

    Who are the "orphans and widows" of your community? What does your church do to help such people? How can you get personally involved in helping?

> And while you are pitiful to the afflicted, see that you are
> courteous toward all men. It matters not in this respect
> whether they are high or low, rich or poor, superior or inferior
> to you. No, nor even whether good or bad, whether they fear
> God or not. Indeed, the mode of showing your courtesy may
> vary, as Christian prudence will direct; but the thing itself is
> due to all; the lowest and worst have a claim to our courtesy.
> —*John Wesley*

14. Proverbs 21:13 is sobering: "Whoever closes his ears to the cry of the poor will himself call out and not be answered" (ESV). God takes our lack of concern for the poor very seriously.

    Reflect on this passage. Do you close your ears to the poor? If so, why? What is one step you can take this week to become more aware of the needs of the poor and hurting in your community?

DIGGING DEEPER

> Moreover, say to the royal house of Judah, "Hear the word of the
> LORD; O house of David, this is what the LORD says: 'Administer
> justice every morning; rescue from the hand of his oppressor the
> one who has been robbed, or my wrath will break out and burn
> like fire because of the evil you have done — burn with no one
> to quench it.' "
>
> — *Jeremiah 21:11 – 12*

Jeremiah 21:11 – 23:8 is only one of many Old Testament passages calling for the combination of justice and righteousness. Justice makes sense
to us, but the concept of righteousness has become so spiritualized that
we sometimes find it hard to get our arms around it. This passage clari-
fies the connection between these biblical terms and more explicitly economic and social issues.

Jeremiah 21:12 connects faith and finances: justice and righteousness
are equated with rescuing the poor and oppressed who have been robbed
and exploited (cf. Jer. 22:3). In contrast, the king's extravagant lifestyle
is described as unjust and unrighteous — to reach what he wants, he
can't avoid stepping on others (Jer. 22:13).

The passage draws an interesting connection between the way we
deal with the poor and the way God deals with us. We tend to assess
ourselves according to the quality of our connections with the rich and
powerful, but God judges us specifically by how we relate to the poor
and oppressed (Jer. 22:4 – 5).

The prophet Hosea writes, "In you the orphan finds mercy" (Hos.
14:3b NRSV). To whom, exactly, does this "you" refer? Who is responsible for meeting the needs of those unable to provide for themselves?

Even during the monarchy, God intended that the king act as his rep-
resentative, executing his will. This ideal, of course, was realized all too
seldom. While the Bible does not address such modern issues as social-
ism, democracy, or the separation of church and state, it is abundantly
clear that God's people are to make sure the needy receive justice. Dutch
statesman and theologian Abraham Kuyper (1837 – 1920) had this to
say on the subject:

> There cannot be two different faiths — one for you and one
> for the poor. The question on which the whole social problem

> really pivots is whether you recognize in the less fortunate, even in the poorest, not merely a creature, a person in wretched circumstances, but one of your own flesh and blood: for the sake of Christ, *your brother*.... Those who are diverted by fear for their money box have no place marching in the ranks with us. This is holy ground, and he who would walk on it must first loosen the sandals of his egotism.

As biblical stewards of our fellow man, we do what we do because our motivations have been transformed from the inside out. We no longer follow the standard operating procedure of looking out for Number One. Jesus' new life in us has reoriented our values, goals, and actions. In effect, Christ has turned the old way on its head, which Luke 6:27–36 vividly portrays.

The great "kingdom reversal" is at work in this passage. The world we live in expects us to live by its standard operating procedure of self-service, self-preservation, and self-fulfillment. But Jesus calls us to a life lived with radically different motives and actions. He calls us to "be perfect, therefore, as your heavenly Father is perfect" (Matt. 5:48), which is to receive and nurture within ourselves the love of God — agape love.

For instance, just as God has not let our hostility toward him turn him against us, so we are to persistently love those hostile toward us. Jesus said, "Love your enemies and pray for those who persecute you" (Matt. 5:44). Imagine how Jesus looked deep into the eyes of those who opposed him to see them as the Father would. Can you and I do less than look into the eyes of our enemies and search for the image of God in them?

By the world's standards, loving those who love you is perfectly understandable. Doing good to those who do you good is just sensible reciprocal business (Matt. 5:46–47). But the kingdom economy has very different ground rules. Those who are children of the Most High God give without reciprocity.

Theologian Miroslav Volf says that if "God is the third party in the relationship between givers and recipients, givers cannot lose. They always receive what they give, and more," for "those who pass gifts on receive more abundantly from the source of all gifts."

When a kingdom steward lives and loves by this mode of operation, the world looks at him or her and sees something different. They see the light (Matt. 5:14) that comes from the Light of the World (John 8:12).

READING RESOURCES

Free of Charge: Giving and Forgiving in a Culture Stripped of Grace, by Miroslav Volf (Grand Rapids: Zondervan, 2005).

Renewing American Compassion: How Compassion for the Needy Can Turn Ordinary Citizens into Heroes, by Marvin Olasky (New York: Free Press, 1996).

Wealth and Poverty, by George Gilder (New York: Basic Books, 1981).

Session Four

CHURCH AND FAMILY

Genesis 2:24; Matthew 13:31 – 33; Ephesians 5:22 – 32

> And let us consider how we may spur one another on toward love and good deeds. Let us not give up meeting together, as some are in the habit of doing, but let us encourage one another — and all the more as you see the Day approaching.
> —*Hebrews 10:24–25*

KEY ISSUE

When you hear the word *institution*, your first thought might be of an old brick building. But institutions are simply the ways that we, as human beings, organize ourselves so that we can have a functional society. Two of the most important social institutions are the family and the church.

Marriage is the oldest human institution, older than government. Created by God, marriage is biblically defined as the union of one husband and one wife, for life (see Lev. 18:22; Mal. 2:13 – 16; Matt. 19:3 – 8; Mark 10:2 – 12; Rom. 1:20 – 28).

But the institution of marriage is under attack. The media frequently suggests that "following your dreams" is more important than sticking to your marriage. Divorce rates in the church rise every year. And we continue to bear the bitter fruit of ongoing social experiments that promote the practice of adultery and encourage homosexual relationships. As stewards of the oldest human institution, we need to lovingly and firmly defend God's moral order for marriage and human sexuality.

Effective stewardship of the family begins with a proper understanding of the distinct roles assigned to the family, the church, and the state. When government takes responsibility for roles that properly belong to parents and churches, there are often unintended consequences. What may have started as a compassionate effort to help those who fall between the cracks of society has led to the weakening of family bonds. And various court rulings have effectively restricted religion to the private sphere, limiting the leavening work of the church in the wider culture. As Christians, we have a stewardship responsibility to lovingly but firmly stand against these developments.

DVD Teaching Notes
The family is fundamental to human civilization

Contract, covenant, and commitment

The church: good for families

The church: good for civilization

One nation under God

GROUP DISCUSSION QUESTIONS

DVD Discussion

1. Michael Miller notes that the institution of marriage is older than the institution of human government. What does this suggest about the proper limits of government in relation to the institution of marriage? Where do you see conflict between these two institutions in contemporary culture?

> No authority or power on earth is inherent but is imposed. Thus there is no natural authority to speak of either on the part of the ruler or of the people. Only God is sovereign.... He is sovereign and gives that authority to whomever he will—sometimes to kings and princes, other times to nobles and patricians, but sometimes also to people as a whole.
>
> —*Abraham Kuyper*

2. Economist Jennifer Roback Morse says, "All of these kind of natural things that parents do with their children are all constructive and productive, and you can't replace that with hired help. You can't replace it with a machine. None of that is an adequate substitute for what mothers and fathers do when they simply love and take care of their children."

Where do you see this trend, the replacement of the parental role, at work in our culture? How does the redefinition of the family and the rearrangement of parental roles affect children?

What are some ways that you personally have experienced this or seen its effects?

> Every advocate of the free market and limited government knows that we are not "free to choose" a prosperous society that has no private property rights. I would add that neither are we free to choose a society in which every generation completely renegotiates its definitions of family relationships, obligations, and virtues. Some familial obligations are inherent in the relationship of parent and child. Some virtues are indispensible.
>
> —*Jennifer Roback Morse*

3. While it is essential that the government respects the God-given responsibility of parents, there may be times when it is necessary for the government to intervene in family affairs. For example, in cases of parental abuse, it may be appropriate for the government to act to protect a child from his or her own parents.

   How can the government protect children in such situations without penalizing all parents for the sins of a few? How can we balance the two sides of this issue?

4. Robert George makes the case that Christianity and the Judeo-Christian worldview have led to greater human rights for all people. Give examples of principles or ideas developed out of the Christian faith that have led to greater human rights.

Many today have forgotten the positive contributions of the Christian faith and now view the church in a very negative light. Why do you think the church is viewed so negatively in our culture? What can Christians do to change this perception?

Bible Exploration

5. Read together Genesis 2:24 and Matthew 19:4–6. It's clear from these verses that marriage is a covenant and a mystery, created by God. Often, however, our culture treats marriage as little more than a convenient social arrangement. As an illustration, take two newly married couples. One of them understands marriage to be a physical and spiritual union created by God, while the other views it as a convenient social arrangement.

How will these two different understandings affect the decisions that are made in these marriages?

Discuss your own understanding of marriage in light of these passages from Scripture.

6. Read Ruth 1:15–18 and 1 Timothy 5:3–8, 16. These and other Scriptures say we are responsible for our families—not only for our children, but for our elderly relatives. In past generations it was common for aging parents to live with their grown children. Why has this become so rare in our society today?

How does our government encourage or discourage our responsibility to care for our families? What types of challenges and sacrifices might be required to care for an aging parent? What types of blessings might come from such care?

7. Read together Romans 12:5; Galatians 3:28; and Colossians 3:11. When we go to a grocery store, restaurant, or movie, we think like consumers and focus on satisfying our needs and desires. As members of God's church, we need to change our thinking and consider not only what we need, but what we can give to others.

Why is this such a hard change for us to make? What are some things we can do to cultivate the attitude that we are members of Christ's body and have stewardship responsibilities toward other members of the body?

8. Stewardship of the God-given institutions of family and church requires faithful commitment. Read together Deuteronomy 7:9; 2 Thessalonians 3:3; 2 Timothy 2:13; and Hebrews 10:23; 13:5–6. Meditating on God's faithfulness can provide comfort and inspire us to be faithful in our own commitments to God and one another. What are some ways God has shown his faithfulness to you through the institutions of family and the church?

Love's not Time's fool, though rosy lips and cheeks
Within his bending sickle's compass come:
Love alters not with his brief hours and weeks,
But bears it out even to the edge of doom.
— *William Shakespeare*

9. In Romans 12:2, Paul says, "Do not conform any longer to the pattern of this world, but be transformed by the renewing of your mind." Children today are bombarded with the message that traditional Christian morality is judgmental and old-fashioned. In such a climate, what do we need to do to help young Christians develop a strong moral vision that is not conformed to "the pattern of this world"?

Living the Truth

10. Some women must raise their children without a husband to help them. These women can take comfort in knowing that God promises to be a father to the fatherless and a protector of widows (see Deut. 10:18; Ps. 68:5).

What can the church do to help single mothers (or single fathers)? What can you do?

11. Close extended family ties can be a means of sharing the wisdom of old age and the energy and optimism of youth. That's another way of saying that grandparents and grandchildren are usually good for each other. It used to be the norm for grandparents to live with their children and grandchildren during retirement years, making intergenerational sharing a natural part of household life. Today that scenario is far from inevitable.

Given this reality, are there still things we can do to encourage intergenerational sharing? How can the church help provide some of these blessings for church members who do not and perhaps cannot have this blessing in their lives?

12. Hebrews 13:4 says that "marriage should be honored by all, and the marriage bed kept pure." What are some of the ways that marriage is dishonored in our culture? What can we do, practically, to honor marriage as an institution?

DIGGING DEEPER

> If anyone does not provide for his relatives, and especially for his immediate family, he has denied the faith and is worse than an unbeliever.
>
> —*1 Timothy 5:8*

God ordained the family unit in part so we can meet one another's needs. The apostle Paul says that anyone who chooses not to provide for members of his household is worse than an unbeliever. Indeed, Paul spends an entire chapter instructing the young pastor Timothy that stewardship begins at home.

John Wesley (1703–1791) had this to say:

> Every man ought to provide the plain necessities of life, both for his own wife and children; and to put them into a capacity of providing these for themselves, when he is gone hence and is no more seen. I say, of providing these; the plain necessities of life; not delicacies; not superfluities—and that by their diligent labor.

The late expository preacher Stephen F. Olford offered this observation:

> In my pastoral counseling I have listened to many stories of tragic circumstances. Husbands have failed their wives, parents have cheated their children, and grown sons and daughters have neglected their widowed mothers or other dependents. Such shortcomings are soundly and solemnly condemned by the Word of God; in fact, such dereliction of duty is described as worse than infidelity.
>
> In light of the foregoing, it is certainly biblical and practical that savings accounts be established and insurance policies be taken out to cover the needs of dependents, emergency requirements, funeral expenses, and so on. Such financial matters should be openly discussed in every Christian household. With an open Bible and in an atmosphere of prayer, our tithes, offerings, expenses, and savings should be surveyed in relation to personal, as well as general, income. Happy and healthy in the Spirit is the family that is united on all these matters. In the last analysis, every one of us is responsible to God in time and accountable to him in eternity (Gal. 6:2–10).

Paul's words indicate that we also must consider what role we should play for extended family members—aunts, uncles, and cousins. Do we have family members who need shelter, housing, companionship, nutrition, and medical care? Are there avenues we can take to help them procure goods and services through whatever private or public means are available to them? Failing that, how can we help them?

Another institution God has entrusted to humans is political government. God appointed the governing authorities as his stewards to protect good and punish evildoers. The public official is described as having been appointed by God as a "servant to do you good" and "an agent of wrath to bring punishment on the wrongdoer" (Rom. 13:4). These descriptions all point to the civil magistrate as one of God's stewards. Ronald J. Sider elaborates on the idea that the government is a good and necessary element of God's created order. "Since persons are communal beings created in the image of the Trinity, we naturally create a variety of different structural institutions," he writes. Government is one of those institutions. "It is not the only or even the most important institution of society, but it is a crucial element of a good society." In short, government "is a gift from God, not an invention of Satan."

Preacher and author John R. W. Stott emphasizes that, while obedience to government is commanded, it must not come before obedience to God:

> The disciples of Jesus are to respect the state, and within limits submit to it, but they will neither worship it, nor give it the uncritical support it covets. Consequently, discipleship sometimes calls for disobedience. Indeed, civil disobedience is a biblical doctrine, for there are four or five notable examples of it in Scripture. It arises naturally from the affirmation that Jesus is Lord. The principle is clear, even though its application may involve believers in agonies of conscience. It is this. We are to submit to the state, because its authority is derived from God and its officials are God's ministers, right up to the point where obedience to the state would involve us in disobedience to God. At that point, our Christian duty is to disobey the state in order to obey God. For if the state misuses its God-given authority, and presumes either to command what God forbids or to forbid what God commands, we have to say "no" to the state in order to say "yes" to Christ.

READING RESOURCES

Being the Body: A New Call for the Church to Be Light in the Darkness, by Charles Colson and Ellen Vaughn (Nashville: Thomas Nelson, 2003).

The Birth of Freedom DVD (Grand Rapids: Acton Media, 2008).

Men and Marriage, by George Gilder (Gretna, La.: Pelican, 1986).

True Sexual Morality: Recovering Biblical Standards for a Culture in Crisis, by Daniel R. Heimbach (Wheaton, Ill.: Crossway, 2005).

FINANCES AND GIVING

Matthew 6:25–34; 1 Timothy 6:6–10

> So do not worry, saying, "What shall we eat?" or "What shall we drink?" or "What shall we wear?" For the pagans run after all these things, and your heavenly Father knows that you need them. But seek first his kingdom and his righteousness, and all these things will be given to you as well.
>
> —*Matthew 6:31–33*

KEY ISSUE

The Bible repeatedly warns us not to obsess over wealth, for the love of money leads to much dissatisfaction, grief, and evil (Matt. 6:25–34; Eccl. 5:10; 1 Tim. 6:6–10; Heb. 13:5).

Because of these stern warnings, some conclude that Christians are called to take vows of poverty. But this isn't what the Bible teaches. Yes, Jesus commanded the rich young ruler to sell everything he had and give it to the poor. And he singled out the poor widow who gave all she had as a model of heroic generosity. But these are the exceptions, not the biblical rule.

The biblical steward is commanded to "give what he has decided in his heart to give, not reluctantly or under compulsion" (2 Cor. 9:7a). We also are instructed to:

- provide financially for our children and elder relatives (2 Cor. 12:14; 1 Tim. 5:4, 8, 16);
- contribute regularly to the needs of the saints, rather than in a single bankrupting swoop of generosity; to show hospitality (Rom. 12:13; Heb. 13:2; 1 Peter 4:9);

- pay honest wages for honest work (James 5:3–5);
- and look after those who cannot provide for themselves (James 1:27).

In short, we are not called to hand over all our wealth to someone else to manage, but rather to manage wisely the wealth God entrusts to us, sharing it ably and well.

DVD TEACHING NOTES

Stewardship involves all that God has entrusted to us

Money as tool versus money as idol

2.5 percent versus 1.6 billion

With the measure you use it will be measured back to you

Keys to successful living financially

GROUP DISCUSSION QUESTIONS

DVD Discussion

1. Ron Blue says, "The key to somebody being a good steward is to come to grips first of all with the reality that God owns it all. And if you really deal with that ... then you realize that every spending decision you make is in reality a spiritual decision."

   If we believed this spiritual truth deep in our bones so that it shaped our every action, what are some specific ways we might behave differently?

   When we give cheerfully, as an act of worship, the very act of giving moves us to lose interest in ourselves and to devote ourselves to God. We may care about how the money that we give is used but that isn't the *reason* we give it. We may appreciate having our gifts acknowledged, but that isn't *why* we give them. In some mysterious way, such giving—motivated only by our love for God—ends up meeting our *own* deep spiritual needs and is intensely satisfying.

   —*Mark Allan Powell*

2. Proverbs says that for lack of counsel, plans fail. As fallible human beings, none of us are completely objective about our own spending plans. Even Ron Blue, a respected financial counselor, shares his personal spending ideas and habits with a trusted friend for accountability. What type of accountability do you have with your own finances?

What practices have you developed in your own life to help you become a better steward of God's resources?

3. Dave Stotts says, "If you're like me, you have a little bit of that eccentric millionaire Howard Hughes in you. One time he was asked, how much is enough? His answer: 'Just a little more.' We have to remind ourselves that happiness is never found in 'a little more.'"

The advertising industry often tries to convince us that we will find happiness in "just a little more" stuff. Share some examples of how you have seen this message in the media.

How have you been affected by this constant barrage of advertising propaganda?

4. Stephen Grabill says the lesson of the rich young ruler is "to be more loyal to Jesus Christ and the claims of Christ than to your possessions, to reprioritize your life around the things that matter." If there were one physical possession in your life that posed a danger of becoming more important to you than it should, what would it be?

Bible Exploration

5. In Acts 20:35 the apostle Paul reminds us of the words of Jesus: "It is more blessed to give than to receive." How has this been true in your own life?

Why do we often have trouble believing this when it comes to giving of our financial resources?

6. Read Matthew 6:19–21, where Jesus teaches that where our treasure is stored, our heart will be found as well. In other words, our spending patterns are often an accurate reflection of our deepest values. If one were to judge solely by your purchases and the way you spend your money, where would they find your heart? What would they say you value?

> The gospel is a gospel of giving and forgiving. We may sum it up in those two words; and hence, when the true spirit of it works upon the Christian, he forgives freely, and he also gives freely. The large heart of God breeds large hearts in men, and they who live upon his bounty are led by his Spirit to imitate that bounty, according to their power.
>
> —*Charles Spurgeon*

7. The Old Testament called on the Israelites to tithe, that is, to give at least 10 percent to the Lord. (The total was actually higher when you take into account various other commands to give, such as almsgiving.) Since the New Testament never explicitly lays down the tithe as a requirement, many Christians have taken this as permission to give substantially less.

Consider the following passages of Scripture. What guidance do these passages offer Christians on the subject of giving? Summarize the point of each verse.

• Psalm 24:1

- 2 Corinthians 9:6

- 2 Corinthians 9:7

- 2 Corinthians 9:8

- 2 Corinthians 9:11

8. Read together 2 Corinthians 12:14; 1 Timothy 5:4; and Luke 12:13–21. What do these passages teach us about keeping a balance between our need to provide for our families and the danger of hoarding wealth? How do you balance your saving with your giving?

Living the Truth

9. With the development of new technologies and changing lifestyles, the distinction between what we "need" and what we "want" has blurred. In many cases, we have labeled something as a "need" that would have been considered a luxury to previous generations or to those living in less-developed countries.

   What standard do you use to determine if something is a "want" or a "need"? Is this a standard that will vary from person to person? Why or why not?

   To what extent is it okay for Christians to take the cultural norm as our own norm, and at what point should we decide to be different from the surrounding culture?

10. Most of us tend to define excessive wealth by choosing a dollar amount that is just beyond what we would ever expect to make, personally. We often fail to realize that people who make far less do the exact same thing, judging *us* excessive by their own standard of living.

What is the danger of this way of thinking? What would be a more fruitful way of approaching the problem of excessive spending?

Are there principles that can apply to our financial stewardship, regardless of our income level? Give some examples.

11. One of our responsibilities is to instill good habits of financial responsibility in our kids. For those of you with children or grand-children, how are you helping them learn to manage finances in a responsible, biblical way? What specific disciplines or habits are you seeking to cultivate in their lives?

> Render thanks unto God, that he hath put you among the givers, and not among the receivers, it being a more blessed thing to give than to receive: that he hath put you among the givers and not the withholders: that he hath given you something to give, and a heart to distribute of your abundance to the needy, and to the furtherance of the establishing of the kingdom of Christ on earth.
>
> *— Thomas Gouge*

12. The New Testament depicts the body of Christ as various parts who are supposed to help and accept help from one another. If you need to speak to someone about your finances or about your attitude toward wealth, take specific steps to bring that about this week. Perhaps a good first step is to seek out, or ask your church leaders to conduct, a class on financial stewardship built around biblical principles. What are some things you would want such a class to cover?

Digging Deeper

> When Jacob awoke from his sleep, he thought, "Surely the LORD
> is in this place, and I was not aware of it." He was afraid and said,
> "How awesome is this place! This is none other than the house
> of God; this is the gate of heaven." ... Then Jacob made a vow,
> saying, "If God will be with me and will watch over me on this
> journey I am taking and will give me food to eat and clothes to
> wear so that I return safely to my father's house, then the LORD
> will be my God and this stone that I have set up as a pillar will be
> God's house, and of all that you give me I will give you a tenth."
> *—Genesis 28:16–17, 20–22*

When the topic of giving comes up, there is a tendency to focus almost
all of our attention on the questions of how much, to whom, and how
often. However, Genesis 28:16–22 provides a healthy reminder that our
starting point should be with the question of why we give at all. Boiled
down to its essentials, giving is worship.

Author Mark Allan Powell elaborates: "The patriarch Jacob experi-
ences God's presence in a dream and, not knowing what else to do, sets
up a stone and pours oil over the top of it (Gen. 28:16–18)." Powell
points out that early Old Testament "people who had been touched by
the goodness of God wanted to worship God, and they did that by taking something that belonged to them and giving it to God in the only
way they knew how." Powell continues:

> God may be pleased, indeed delighted, with us even if we are
> giving the wrong amount, even if [we] are giving to unworthy
> or inappropriate causes. As we learn more about stewardship,
> of course, we will want to grow in those respects. We can
> spend a lifetime trying to find better ways of fulfilling God's
> expectations. But, for starters, our principal concern in giv-
> ing should not be where to give, or how to give, or how much
> to give. First, let us focus on the *why*. If we give with hearts
> full of devotion for the God who loves us, then the questions
> of *where* and *how* and *how much* will work themselves out
> in time.

In 2 Corinthians 8:1–7 the apostle Paul refers to giving in the con-
text of grace. What is the grace of giving? Pastor and author Gene Getz

discusses how the Macedonians exhibited giving that was at once spontaneous, eager, and sacrificial:

> There was no coercion. Their decisions were "entirely on their own" (2 Cor. 8:3). In fact, Paul said, "they urgently pleaded with us for the privilege of sharing in this service to the saints" (2 Cor. 8:4). They were eager to help meet other Christians' material needs.... Their response was far beyond what [Paul] had expected. But a more significant reason than human need prompted this sacrificial generosity. They gave "themselves first to the Lord"—which is the larger context in which Christians are to use their material possessions. It involves, first of all, presenting our bodies as "living sacrifices, holy and pleasing to God" (Rom. 12:1).

Paul holds up their example of gracious giving as a sign of their maturity in the body of Christ.

Stewardship theologian T. A. Kantonen provides another striking example of the grace of giving, one he learned about during a seminar on Christian social ethics:

> Dr. Otto A. Piper, then a professor at Princeton Theological Seminary, told us this incident from his post-war work of collecting funds for the relief of the needy in German universities. Dr. Piper described to a group of Princeton students the conditions of abject poverty in which German students were struggling and asked his hearers to do what they could to help. The next morning a young married couple, both graduate students, came into Dr. Piper's office, placed three hundred dollars on his desk and said, "We heard your talk last night. We have talked it over, and this is our answer to your appeal." He was astonished at the generosity of the gift and said, "Are you sure you can afford this much?" They replied, "It is true that our resources are quite limited. We had saved this money to buy some things that we need. We could use a new refrigerator, and the old car is getting to the point where it should be traded in for a new one. But after all, God has been good to us and we can get along. Those people in Germany need this money much more than we do. We would rather have the joy of giving it to them."

Second Corinthians 9:6–7 (ESV) is rich in wisdom about giving. Let's linger over three segments in particular:

Whoever sows sparingly will also reap sparingly, and whoever sows bountifully will also reap bountifully ...

Stephen F. Olford explains:

> The farmer understands that the proportion of his reaping will be determined by the proportion of his sowing.... This principle is true in all areas of Christian experience, especially in the area of giving. The believer recognizes that giving is not a question of scattering, but of sowing and that—since all giving constitutes a challenge to faith—it is not a contribution, but an investment.

Each one must give as he has made up his mind, not reluctantly or under compulsion ...

Theologian Mark Allan Powell maintains that beyond giving a reasonable, proportionate pledge of support for one's own congregation, there is room for joyful, sacrificial giving:

> Then our offerings can be somewhat sporadic, spontaneous, unpredictable, and reflective of our varying levels of enthusiasm and areas of commitment. They can be Spirit-led: we are free to follow our conscience and our intuition in deciding how much to give and when to give it. There is great joy in such giving, for we are not merely fulfilling a basic responsibility but, in truth, are opening our hearts to the goodness of God. It is in such giving that we become generous people. It is in such giving that we become grateful people. Indeed, it is in such giving that we become godly people.

God loves a cheerful giver.

God delights in our cheerful giving. He wants us to find joy. He even commands us to rejoice (Phil. 4:4). What command could be a greater pleasure to obey than that one? But if we don't give, we're robbing ourselves of the source of joy God instructs us to seek. As Randy Alcorn says:

The more we give, the more we delight in our giving—and the more God delights in us. Our giving pleases us. But more importantly, it pleases God. This doesn't mean we should give only when we're feeling cheerful. The cheerfulness often comes during and after the act of obedience, not before it. So don't wait until you feel like giving—it could be a long wait! Just give and watch the joy follow.

READING RESOURCES

Generous Living: Finding Contentment through Giving, by Ron Blue with Jodie Berndt (Grand Rapids: Zondervan, 1997).

Money, Possessions, and Eternity, by Randy Alcorn (Wheaton, Ill.: Tyndale, 1989).

The New Master Your Money, by Ron Blue with Jeremy White (Chicago: Moody, 2004).

The Total Money Makeover: A Proven Plan for Financial Fitness, by Dave Ramsey (Nashville: Thomas Nelson, 2003).

ABOUT THE AUTHORS

JONATHAN WITT, PhD, is a research fellow at the Acton Institute and the author of *A Meaningful World* (with Benjamin Wiker). Witt also wrote or cowrote scripts for documentaries that have aired on PBS, TBN, and Fox Business.

AMANDA WITT, PhD, is a freelance writer who has been interviewed about family issues by *Focus on the Family* magazine. Her essays, poetry, and fiction have appeared in such places as *Touchstone, Christianity and Literature, Windhover, New Texas,* and in a collection of mystery stories edited by bestselling novelist Jeffery Deaver.

THE WITTS also wrote the scripts for the *Effective Stewardship* DVD series. They live on a small farm outside Grand Rapids, Michigan, where they homeschool their three children and try to keep the natural food chain among dog, cat and chicken from reasserting itself.

NIV Stewardship Study Bible

Discover God's Design for Life, the Environment, Finances, Generosity, and Eternity

New International Version

The *NIV Stewardship Study Bible* uses a variety of engaging features to lead individuals through a comprehensive study of what it means to be managers entrusted with the resources of God. Through 366 Exploring Stewardship notes, profiles of individuals, notes on challenges to stewardship, quotes on stewardship from respected Christians throughout the ages, and other articles and helps, the *NIV Stewardship Study Bible* projects a positive picture of the privilege that we have to manage what God has given us to his glory and to the building of his kingdom.

More than just money, this Bible emphasizes stewardly responsibility in all areas of life, including relationships, creation care, money management, institutions, and caring for the poor, among other areas. It's been pulled together with the purpose of changing perceptions about what the word "stewardship" means—not something intended to be draining and guilt-inducing, but rather motivating, empowering, and uplifting.

The *NIV Stewardship Study Bible* has been endorsed by Crown Ministries, Dave Ramsey, Good $ense Ministry, the Barnabas Foundation, Prison Fellowship, and various other programs and ministries that seek to encourage responsible stewardship among Christians. This Bible will be a natural "next step" for individuals and groups who benefit from these ministries and take part in their programs.

ISBN 978-0-310-94847-6

NOTES:

NOTES:

NOTES:

NOTES:

Share Your Thoughts

With the Author: Your comments will be forwarded to the author when you send them to *zauthor@zondervan.com*.

With Zondervan: Submit your review of this book by writing to *zreview@zondervan.com*.

Free Online Resources at
www.zondervan.com

Zondervan AuthorTracker: Be notified whenever your favorite authors publish new books, go on tour, or post an update about what's happening in their lives.

Daily Bible Verses and Devotions: Enrich your life with daily Bible verses or devotions that help you start every morning focused on God.

Free Email Publications: Sign up for newsletters on fiction, Christian living, church ministry, parenting, and more.

Zondervan Bible Search: Find and compare Bible passages in a variety of translations at www.zondervanbiblesearch.com.

Other Benefits: Register yourself to receive online benefits like coupons and special offers, or to participate in research.

ZONDERVAN®
.com